WIND
DAUGHTER

God be with you
Eileen Curteis, ssa

WIND
DAUGHTER

Eileen Curteis

Ekstasis Editions

Canadian Cataloguing in Publication Data
Curteis, Eileen,
Wind daughter

Poems
ISBN 1-896860-43-5

I. Title.
PS8555.U84W56 1998 C811'.54 C98-911043-5
PR9199.3.G8257W56 1998

Acknowledgements:
Some of these poems have appeared in the following books, periodicals, journals and newspapers: *Island Catholic News, Prairie Messenger, Sisters Today, L'Antenne, Grail, In The Desert Sun, paperplates, Forward In The Spirit.*

I would like to thank Susan McCaslin for her wonderful support and editorial skills in helping me bring this book to completion, to Frank Tierney for his introduction and belief in me as a poet, to Jason and Mel for the cover photo, to Diane Tolomeo adnd Richard Renshaw for their excellent blurbs, to my friends who contributed the photography, and to my publisher, Richard Olafson, for his deep and joyful spirituality.

Published in 1998 by:
Ekstasis Editions Canada Ltd.   Ekstasis Editions
Box 8474, Main Postal Outlet   Box 571
Victoria, B.C. V8W 3S1   Banff, Alberta ToL oCo

THE CANADA COUNCIL | LE CONSEIL DES ARTS
FOR THE ARTS | DU CANADA
SINCE 1957 | DEPUIS 1957

Wind Daughter has been published with the assistance of a grant from the Canada Council and the Cultural Services Branch of British Columbia.

INTRODUCTION

Genuine feeling from intense suffering experienced by a poet frequently produces beautiful and convincing poems, as in this volume by Sister Eileen Curteis. The reader need not have met Sister Eileen to recognize her pain and her joy because they are the pains and joys of all humanity; she speaks for each of us and captures our human journey from innocence to experience, from suffering to joy, from material preoccupation to spiritual reconciliation, and from discord to harmony in God through Christ.

This is a voice of Christian existentialism in the tradition of Karl Jaspers and Jacques Maritain. There is no defeat. Personal turmoil is exposed and tender and vulnerable self-esteem is buffeted and pounded until the speaker withdraws to her "corner" ("Small's World"), but "In the morning / Small puts seeds / on the window. / Birds come / and she sees them," and by the poem's end "Small / is unafraid of Small." Corners, cages, islands, and impenetrable walls are used to represent hiding places, traps and hurdles, but those are always temporary on this journey because, as the speaker in the title poem exclaims, "I want to be real! Make me real!" and Mother Wind replies, "Suffering will make you real...Go now to the others," ("Wind Daughter"). The "others" are you and I and our brothers and sisters throughout the world. And these poems console and encourage us: the aged, the ill, the lonely, the afraid, the handicapped, the unloved, the confused, the rejected, and we are lifted to accept and grow with our personal challenges because "hardship / is something [we must] walk through," ("Tough As Steel"), and we will find that "There is nowhere [we] cannot fly, now!" ("Fog Lift").

The human paradox, fearful vulnerability and courageous resilience, is expressed tenderly by the "Funny little girl....flattened ...lonely... heart stitched up on the wall / and face scarred /..can a lame girl walk blindly /..I see you walking now with the body of a lamb," ("Little Lamb Girl"). The lamb is one of the many Christian symbols in a volume which includes among many others the wind, representing the Holy Spirit, and the kite as symbol of Christ's cross.

5

One of the most frequent and appropriately so, is the bird as symbol of freedom: getting to know yourself is what it's all about self realization is the wound in the bird that soars," ("Self Discovery").

The final poem, "Self Portrait," expresses the heart of the volume: "the rope whose shreds you live by. / Be for us, a sign of delivery, / a Stream, running through the city of our concerns." These poems express the universal journey that parallels Christ's: He loved, was rejected, was tortured, was crucified, and resurrected to heal the world; this is a resurrection volume.

Dr. Frank M. Tierney,
Professor of English,
University of Ottawa.

CONTENTS

For mom and dad

Lifelong friends

Photography Acknowledgements:

Wind Daughter —Dorothy Haegert
Small's World —Lonnie Murphy
Fire Woman —Lonnie Murphy
Fear Bellows —Lonnie Murphy
Little Lamb Girl —Lonnie Murphy
Rebuilding The Ruins —Lonnie Murphy
Kite That Sets You Free —Lonnie Murphy
Blessed Laughter —Barb Lyall
June Day —Jason Curteis
Hope Is —Jason Curteis
The Girl Called Worry —Jason Curteis
Fog Lift —Jason Curteis
Tough As Steel —Jason Curteis
True Identity —Jason Curteis
Orange Valley In The Foothills —Peter Gubbels
Resting Place —Peter Gubbels
In Defence Of Animals, In Defence Of Humans —Peter Gubbels
The Return Of Spring —Peter Gubbels
Celebrate Life —Milla Gubbels
Mother Daughter Love —Tom Curteis
Home Of Acceptance —Dan Christian
Shy People's Blood —Dan Christian
Lonely Stance —Dan Christian
Flute Player —Dan Christian
Autumn's Crunch —Bill Broughton
Dad's Aging Silhouette —Page Wheatley
In Tribute to the Loon —Page Wheatley
Delighting In The Transformation Of My Cottage —Page Wheatley
The Call Of Carla —Colleen Hankenberg
Burial Of The Son Of Man —Pauline Cormier
Self Discovery —Bengt Kangasiemi
The Bigger Brighter World —Glenn Ware
Breakthrough —Wendy Currie
Magnet Woman —Derek B. Bollen
Self Portrait —Joyce Harpell

Attempts have been made to locate the photographers
but unfortunately they remain unknown:
Sun Of A New Day
Childhood Revisited And Healed
Winter Stamina
Brutal Waters
Straightened Tree Gone Radiant
Detachment —*Roadway To Happiness*

WIND DAUGHTER

She stood there, a small shred of a thing
as the wind tore into her without mercy.
"Oh Mother Wind," she cried,
"in the heart of a sobbing tree
you bring rain upon me."
"I do that," she said,
"for without this burden
how else can the torn face
of a rag doll get ripped?"

"But Mother Wind," I cried,
"I want to be real! Make me real!"
"Suffering will make you real," she said.
"Just listen to the harsh voice
of a howling wind
and know you can't always
stop the hand that hits you, not always."

"I love you, Mother Wind," I said,
"but you tug hard
at the roots of my knotted hair
and like the slit of a cold knife
going into me
it hurts where you enter."
"Yes, my child," she said.
"It hurts where I enter.
Pain always hurts."

Grief knew no words
and I was silent before her.
"Wind daughter," she said, "you are real.
This last ache has made you real.
Go now to the others."

SMALL'S WORLD

I

Small
is a little girl
who lived sometime
before the war was over
but for Small
the war was never over.
It was just beginning.
One day
Small told her friend:
"When war comes
do not remove these hornets
from my song birds
in the trenches
but let me hear in them
the thunder of my own bullets.
Then teach me courage
how to die
kissing the lips of my toad."

II

Small starts out early
but in the big world
Small gets crushed easily.
Small hates death.
Small hates life.
Small hates everything.
Small is never big.
Small is always small.
Death is small,
as small as Small.

III

Small goes to school.
Small hurts.
Small hides.
Small goes into a corner.
Small sees no one.
No one sees Small.
Small is small,
and death is small,
as small as Small.

IV

It's dark
in Small's world.
Everything is dark.
The food is dark.
The bed is dark.
Small fears the dark!
Small fears everything!

V

Small smiles.
Small sings.
But Small doesn't know
why she does these things.
Small you see
can see no sky,
Small you see
only wants to die.

VI

Small never grows big.
But big grows small.
Small pushes her way
up the stairs
and falls less often
when she gets there.
At the top
Small changes.
Small likes to change.
Small sees things differently.

VII

In the morning
Small puts seeds
on the window.
Birds come
and she sees them.
At night
she closes the door
and it is light
in her room.
People come
and she lets them in.
Small is growing big.

VIII

Small likes to be big.
But Small
is never too big.
Small likes people.
People like Small.
Small goes out.
Small comes in.
Small
is unafraid of Small.

JUNE DAY

In my kitchen
I stopped despairing
the day when the dead song
of a whipped bird left me.

It was a June day
when the wasps
flew in at the window
and not one of them
stung me,
a June day
when the weakened bird
got lifted
and the rose
stuck out its stem
for the first time.

A day like today
where I rejoice and give thanks
that in my kitchen
hope rises like steam
as I burst through yet another year.

ORANGE VALLEY IN THE FOOTHILLS

All you soft-spoken stallions
with your raggy hooves —
    Come
from your mountain ravines;
    come
to this orange valley
in the foothills.

Oh tall, spindly ones
    sing,
    hum,
    dance,
fly with your thistles
in the breeze.

Sleep not
on the stubble
of your childhood memory.
Carry no nettle
just be yourself in the wind!

Resting Place

After the whirlwind of peoples,
cars, busses, city streets,
brakes jarring, tires squealing,
horns honking,
I'd give anything
to lie down in a field of daisies
snuggled into the pajamas of the earth.

Propped up
on a pillow of green moss
I'd yawn at the moon
and laugh at the sun.
I'd count stars
as they twinkled
and with the whizzing of the wind
I'd go spinning like a top,
into the first chimney I came to.

I'd loosen my limbs
and dangle my hair
and call it home just to be there.

Sun Of A New Day

I can remember when it was spring
and how I devised this umbrella
for the first time
months before the avalanche actually came.

People were like robins then,
crowding into my trees,
perching with their feathers on me.
Only sometimes, they became crows,
ravens, scavengers,
gluttonous for the worms
I could not give them.

Now I live inside my shelter.
In the drought season
winter passes through me
like a cyclone in the spring.

This time
I pretend it is not rejection
but a vulture eating me.
Nobody sees that I die, but I do die.

At midnight a light flickers.
Picking up the scraps of my body
I cry out for the sun of a new day!
In the stillness of night,
a Voice whispers, "Go!" and I go!
I do not look back
to see how the skin gets ripped.
I just go and I go and I go!

HOPE IS

Hope is a fuzzy flower
      pushing its way into my hand
      because it loves me.
Hope is sound sleep
      after the rain stops dripping
      on the metal.
Hope is a cat
      licking its wound better.
Hope is the thorn you remove
      from the wing of a sparrow.
Hope is the yardstick you use
      to measure the growth of the beans.
Hope is seeing
      the last banana split going down
      and knowing there'll be another.
Hope is a girl coming back from Mayo
      after the transplant's in.
Hope is a window
      with clean air in a crowded room.
Hope is a flashlight
      that turns the heart over so you can see.
Hope is a balloon waiting to be filled
      with helium for Timmy's birthday.
Hope is the bike under the big bow
      you find at the foot of a Christmas tree.
Hope is the cadillac a rich man disposes of
      so the poor can be fed.
Hope is a brand new daffodil
      growing out of a piece of white rock
      in the coldest part of Alaska.
Hope is going up on a ferris wheel
      with your hands held out to the sky.
Hope is hot soup on the table
      when there's no work for anyone.

Hope is a pianist
     passing over the notes of a song
     for the first time.
Hope is the seeing eye dog
     leading the blind woman home.
Hope is a wedding ring
     poking its finger out of a woman's glove.
Hope is a bright light
     in a dark hole you can't get out of.
Hope is the buzz of a hummingbird
     winging its way upward.
Hope is a tunnel
     with an exit to the moon.
Hope is a monk praying
     with his hands on a golden tree.
Hope is a giant panda
     that promises to hug you
     even when the stuffing's gone.
Hope is a ladder
     that keeps on going when you stop.
Hope is a dream you have;
     at the end of your destination
     an elevator will take you there.

FIRE WOMAN

Blessed be the rose
   that falls once too often
   she shall see God.
Blessed be her body, the scarecrow,
   that brings forth life from the tomb.
   She shall be the mother of many.
Blessed be her spirit.
   She shall bring forth stars from a stone
   and no one shall go hungry from her.
Blessed be the air that floats in
   at her window.
   It shall hoist her up like a sail.
Blessed be the River that springs up
   like a faucet in her.
   It shall gush forth like a stream.
Blessed the woman, who warms her feet
   on the coals of this Fire,
   she shall be heated from within!

THE GIRL CALLED WORRY

Locked in a cupboard
hiding on a shelf
Worry is a fidgety girl
who can't do things right.

In the morning she dresses herself
but the clothes don't fit.
Worry is slim.
Worry is fat.
Worry is never what she wants to be.

With feet too big for her
Worry goes shopping
and the groceries tumble.
Worry trips.
Worry falls.
Worry never goes anywhere
without breaking things.

At school
Worry is the timid little goose girl
who sits at the farthest end of the room.
Worry can't think.
Worry can't talk.
Worry can't do anything.
Worry sits there wondering who Worry is.

One day Worry gets sick
but the doctors don't know that.
Nobody can make Worry well.
Only Worry can.

Back home
Worry crawls out of the box she was in.
Worry breathes. Worry lives.
Worry was never meant to worry.

CHILDHOOD REVISITED AND HEALED

I want to go back and love
the shadow of that small girl
running through
a crooked patch of the earth,
to tell her
that instead of a straight path
the road ran sideways through her.

I want her to know
that I remember the time
when it was cold out
and she didn't deserve to be there.
I loved her then,
but like a thin, shelterless tree
I was not ready
to put my arms around her.

I want to go back to that small,
loveable girl
to tell her to come in out of the rain
up out of the muddy flats
onto the dry forested land.
I want to say to her,
little ice daughter
with the rain-pierced face
of a sun girl
I never disowned you then.
I would never disown you now.

And when the last wind shatters you
I want you to come out
of this blackened sky
wearing white.
I want you to come home to yourself
you, sun daughter of an earth woman,
you, pink bud,
climbing through the green clump
of your loveliness
you, child of a woman
I have grown to love,
I want you to come home to yourself.

HOME OF ACCEPTANCE

In my home
I shall accept anyone
on my carpet —
    cats with claws,
    moose with antlers,
    children with lice,
there shall be no distinctions.

We will not count
the number of books
we have read
or the places we have been
nor will we find the solution
in the headlines
as to why we have come.

We will just sit together
in this room
and pause
as if going nowhere.

Dad's Aging Silhouette

Featherless creature
gone ugly in the mirror
dad reminds me
of the girl I used to be.

Squashed down
like a worm
dad always made a point
of seeing something lovely in me.
At dinner
he would say,
scrunched up lily
in the field,
you really are beautiful!

Dad always defended me.
Even at school
when children called me
wet skunk
dripping in your poo
dad assured me
there never was
a smelly bone in my body!

He saw the good in everyone
and, now,
poor dad
with heart drooped over my shoulder
is as good as he ever was.

MOTHER DAUGHTER LOVE

Sometimes I see
a young girl in the bedroom
clamouring for white flowers
when she can't have any
and I say that woman is me.

Put a period on her
and she becomes a small dot
in a dark room
crying "mother!"
but there is no mother
only zero
at the end of a ruler
the place where mother stops
and she begins.

As individual as we were
the geography
of mother's face
curved in at the edges
as did mine.

We were alike
in many ways,
small of stature
with breasts
the size of a pea,
only mine were smaller.

Fretting over silly things,
like appearances,
we'd end up with prune juice
in the mustard
and say it's all dad's fault.

Make no apologies, mom,
soft dust
in the mouth
gets cleaned out
after the rain.

Autumn's Crunch

Happiness
has to be more
than a wooden doll
or a stuffed scarecrow,
more than the flat bounce
of a coin
or the rude push of a person,
more than a girl
calling "hollow, hollow."

In the worst devastation
happiness has to be picked up
like a crocus in the spring
or a crunched out leaf in the fall.
It cannot exist otherwise.

FEAR BELLOWS

We may have skin
the colour of rainbows
but in our off season
we shut down,
the air thickens,
we thicken.

We do not like the abyss
we are leaning into
that shuddering
middle-aged woman
or man
on the black edge of nowhere.
We do not like it!

In us,
the wild wolf bellows
fear me not,
but we do fear!

BLESSED LAUGHTER

Laughter
is a yellow face
with a frown turned upward.
It never pouts at anyone.
You may go in search of her
but like the curly tail
of a pink pig
rolling down a hill
she must come freely
as the wind bursting into you
or not at all.

At anytime of day
she's the white candle
that brightens up our dull world.
She puts serious things
into perspective
and like a black seal
dancing on her toes
at midnight
she makes everything wonderful!

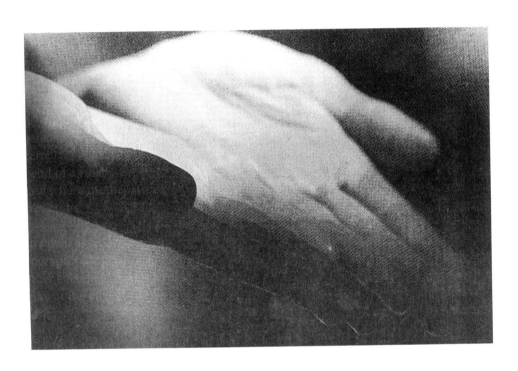

SHY PEOPLE'S BLOOD

You who avoid my island
why do you say I am a leper,
a scab, a sore?
Can you not see me
sitting on the far edge
of the fringe outside you?
I am not the only shy person here.
There are others like me
marred by the black mark
of your indifference.

Unlike you, our words come clumsily,
stuck to the paper.
Sometimes we sit awkwardly
like the dry well of a parched tongue.
We say nothing.
Falling apart like a broken pencil
nobody sees our loneliness
but we are lonely.

At night it is the same thing.
Nobody sees the thorn
in the pillow we sleep on.
We are worlds apart, now,
each in our separate beds.
It is no secret
we are shyly,
beautifully, wonderfully made.
It is for you our hands bleed!

WINTER STAMINA

I shall always be
a winter lilac to you
who look at me
as though I were the last
of the dormant walnuts.

When you crack my world
bring it to nothing
with your heel
sleet gathers me
into its rainy season.

Even in the coldest weather
I do not fold easily.

FOG LIFT

I've left you
and I'm going somewhere, now.
I'm in a car, a steel grey one.
I'm travelling to the city
north of me.
It's an enormous big one, too big,
for a small person to be here
but I am here!

Feeling like an object misplaced
I go into the stores.
I get lost in the furniture.
A man hands me a plastic flower
and I buy it.
I don't like plastic flowers
but I buy it from him.

Later that day
I'm on an island.
I go drifting, drifting.
I don't know why I drift
but I do drift.

Finally, the fog lifts
and I see my way
through to the other side.
I'm making headway, now,
travelling in a jet with my specs on.
This time I don't need anyone
to tell me counterfeit is counterfeit.
I just know pleasing people
or giving the man what he wants
is like selling me an artificial blanket
I can't sleep on.
There is nowhere I cannot fly, now.

BRUTAL WATERS

Buried
deep within you
a shipwreck
known only
to the winds of the sea.

TOUGH AS STEEL

A butterfly of sorts
she comes stomping
out of her frail delicate wings.

Frost bitten in winter
she grows soft petals
tough as steel.

Rains come,
winds blow,
blizzards fall,
there is nothing
she can't withstand.

Like pinched skin
or burnt grass
in a stubby field
hardship
is something she walks through.

58

LITTLE LAMB GIRL

Funny little girl,
with the big dint of a lifetime
all around you,
how does it feel to be flattened?

Is it lonely there,
little girl,
with heart stitched up on the wall
and face scarred,
falling hard
against the wings of your body?
Is it lonely there?

And what about the bent stick
in the stub of your mind?
Can a lame girl
walk blindly with it?
Can she?

And when night falls like a cushion
do you stab it, little girl,
like a hook
or do you say,
fierce things be gentle on me?

Ah yes, little girl,
little woolly girl
with the injured twig,
when night falls like a cushion
I see you walking now
with the body of a lamb.
I see you walking.

Rebuilding The Ruins

Despair is not the only hole
in my doughnut.
Hungry
I cough up the dust
that clogs me.

For too long, now,
I've been living in houses
without furniture, table or chairs;
no food on the counter, either,
just empty canisters
reminding me
starvation
like rust in the mouth
is the disease I suffer from.

Sometimes that's all it takes -
a disease in the mouth.
That way a woman gets killed
by her inordinate desires.
The whole house gets broken in
and, then, she blooms up
like a flower
a woman
not unlike my own woman
putting herself back together
like the fragile, breakable parts
of a jigsaw.

KITE THAT SETS YOU FREE

Adam committed the first sin
then Eve
then me!
How foolish
to think God sits there
drooling like a dog
waiting to pounce on me
everytime I say an unkind word.

I don't believe
what I was told
when I was little -
"white sheep go to heaven
black sheep don't,
be good
mommy loves you,
do as teacher says,
sit up straight in the pew
it's Sunday,
and don't let God see you
chewing that wad of gum!"

Ridiculous!
And, yet, here I am
a brittle bird still trapped
in the warped wood of my anatomy
removing the last of these nails.

In my church
there'll be no more rules,
no more dogmas,
just God
putting a kite
on my splintered tongue
letting me fly thorn free!

THE CALL OF CARLA

One day the cloud uncovered a rainbow.
Carla was in it
teaching the children
how it all had happened.
"Schools were made to learn in,"
she said,
"but not everyone can fly a kite.
Some trail the string
and the building confines them.
Envision, now,
an unusual wind,
birds flying in at the window,
and you taking flight
through the broken glass."

Of course, we never soar
through space in this way
but Carla tells us
the child is an imaginary creature
who needs to be stirred
like the wind and the rain and the trees
and, somewhere,
there is a Carla in all of us.

Whenever we chase rainbows, smell bacon,
suck lollipops, swing on swings,
pick dandelions, climb trees,
whenever we do these things
Carla does them, too.

Carla sits, Carla waits.
Carla is the imaginary creature
in all of us
who needs to be stirred
like the wind and the rain and the trees.
Carla! Carla! Carla!

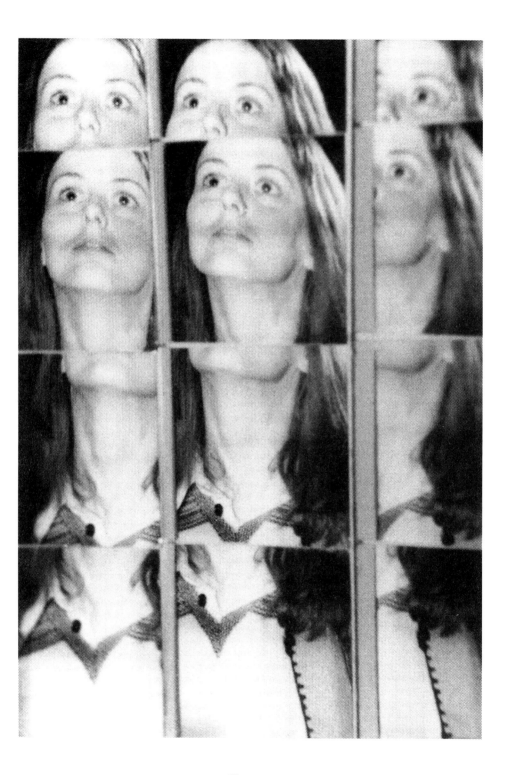

SELF DISCOVERY

Guilt grows best
when left to ripen on a tree.
Just look at yourself -
figs, prunes, walnuts,
cabbage, cauliflower,
it takes a long time
to decipher who you are.

It's not easy
being a mixed-up person
but, then, who said life is easy.
Sometimes I listen to news reporters
and they say
razors among other things
are the cause of disappointment.
For me, though,
there is more loneliness
in a daisy without purpose
than in a woman
who stumbles on her own pebbles.
I say this
because I have stumbled on mine.

Before coming to this conclusion
I've done a lot of living and dying
and I think I could rightly say
getting to know yourself
is what it's all about
or as a poet would say
self realization
is the wound in the bird that soars.

STRAIGHTENED TREE GONE RADIANT

When I learned to accept
the wart, the mole,
the obstruction on my face
only then could I say
this field is beautiful,
that ocean is lovely,
but truly
I could not have said it
without you, my friends,
who have made my whole self
loveable.

In my weakness
never once did you call me
a deformity in the rain.
Instead,
you said I was the drizzle
that brings new life
to the trees
and, so, I shot up in your presence
as one who knew
what it meant to be straightened.

TRUE IDENTITY

Tell me,
are you a butterfly
or a spider
and what face do you wear,
yours or the world's?

And, why,
if the sky is blue
conceal yourself in the shadows?
For centuries
people have been doing this
and saying:
   "Love
   locked up in a cage
   is a cocoon
   that flies by night."
But why conceal your beauty?

Masks
are the starvation guard rails
you wear.
Only you can remove them.

Burial Of The Son Of Man

When he died the world was filled
with the crying sound of a crushed bird.
It rose up in anger and said,
"First, you kill the innocent Son
of a mother.
Then, with the last portion of his blood
you murder him
like a rat in the graveyard."

As others recalled it,
there were no words in the silent wind
of this clear-eyed messiah,
only tender compassion
the inward gaze of a bud that had fallen.

Still others said,
it was in the year of plague when he came
tall, and yellow-robed,
a quiet strong figure
whose sojourn would be brief among us.

In the villages, they said,
he cut the brambles from under them,
and usually entered from the back door
with a thorn in his finger
and a blade in his side
but above all he was tender.

In the towns, they revered him
like a prophet
but on the outskirts
hailed him as an outlaw of the people.
The poor, he never exposed
but Pharisees
he chiselled into a stone
they threw at him.

As for the mother, she went home
grieving the loss of her Son;
three days later
they saw her walking joyfully
and with the pierced skull of a martyr
they said she had born pain well.

In Tribute To The Loon

To form one's own lyric
and then
to be a friend
of the loon
because it is your own song
you hear.

Is not this
the beauty
of your weird destiny,
the pierced loneliness
with which you fly?

And what is joy
if not the echo
of your melancholy years
the shrill cry
of the bird within you.

THE BIGGER BRIGHTER WINDOW

Candles look best
in dark cellars.
They are the breeding ground
of the flame
that lets you see.

For the most part
we create our own houses
without windows.
We see
only what we want to see —
rats, spiders,
elephants with long tails,
urine on the face of a mouse —
the attributes
of our own declining empire.

But why
look in the mirror this way?
You could be different
less heavy
like a basement
pulled up
by the wisp of a string.

In the end
everything will be made easy
even death on a trolley
so wheel yourself in!

In Defense Of Animals,
In Defense Of Humans

Black tack
under my bum
who wants this kind of secret
kept hidden?

"Not I!" said colt,
with heart threshed down to the floor.
"Not I!" said pony,
with pants pulled down to the ground.
"Not I!" said deer,
with mouth swollen into a wound.
"Not I!" said squirrel,
with shame shoved up my navel.
"Not I!"

Let it be said
what animals know
we know.

Scape-goats
are prisoners of society.
They live in green meadows
behind uncaged walls
of mongrels.
It is not they who die
but we
who fail to count the stars
in their midst!

DETACHMENT --
ROADWAY TO HAPPINESS

Travelling
in my zero climate
you would not be
so sure
of the spoke in your wheel.

You may say to your bicycle:
    Routes are made to follow.
    Paths are made to see.
But I would tell you:
    There is more certainty
    in a woman without food
    who waits
    not knowing why
    on the blunt edge
    of a can opener.

With or without the lid
it doesn't really matter.
Happiness, she says,
is the region within you.

The Return Of Spring

I have never hated anything before
but somehow
your coldness is getting to me.
Like most good people
the moment ice reaches me,
your ice,
I detest it
as the worst enemy
my skin can encounter.

Still, you have the power
to melt me.
I cannot say when
or how this will happen
but when it does happen
I will welcome you
as the fresh bloom
of the first one into me.

LONELY STANCE

She came into our world
something like an orchid
fragilely beautiful
but exotically different
a stranger always,
she ached to be born
in some new way
where the distance of touch
would no longer mean
having to be destroyed
by someone holding her.

BREAKTHROUGH

I love my insects
but through the years
I have learned
there is more freedom
in the jagged edge
of my open can
than in the sterility
of your closed lid.

So why guard yourself
against the impossible?
Only shallow answers come
from containers
like these.

What matters is:
not the glass
but that the jar
be broken.

Magnet Woman

Wise woman
intimate
in your ways of knowing
out of the deep dark woods
you came
with your honey pot
loving the blemishes
out of me.

What did I care about
my poor country, then?
Maps, locations, compasses,
what were these to me
when you were my destination?

In you
I sensed danger —
seagulls with swans
brambles with lilies —
and like a magnet
I was drawn to you.

Obedience had taught me
not to tangle my skirt
never to tangle my skirt
but you said,

"Forget the rules.
Nobody lives by them anyway.
And, moreover,
when you're finished experimenting
with all the clothing there is
you can be beautiful
even in the material
of a messy rag."

Inside the room, her room,
I peered in
at the burnt hands and face
of a woman I knew to be me.
I could not say
whether it was her silence
or mine -
whoever it was it invaded me
like the mystery
of a black spook.

"I am one,
 I am many!" she said.
"Become like me!
 Fire, wind, hail!"

Delighting In The Transformation
Of My Cottage

I can't go on living this way,
off the slime of things;
there has to be something bigger
and better
than the hut I was shut into.

Today,
I'm going to dismantle my rocker;
it creaks with me in it.
The rickety old porch
that, too, will be replaced
by a patio of sorts.

The kitchen
is an old dump of a place.
Blinds never get pulled up
and it needs a paint job
other than black!
I'll see to that in the summer.

As for the floors
you can put a dirty finger
through them
and never find a broom anywhere.
So much for the wax this season!

The roof leaks.
Walls are cracked.
Soot hangs down from the chimney.
It's anything but a dream house
in here.

I'm going fishing in the fall.
By then, I'll have a house
with doors opening onto the lawn.
You won't recognize the garden
with flowers in it.
They'll not be weeds
like the ones I planted.

When you come
there'll be birds on the fence,
sleeping birds that will waken me
from the dream I was in.

CELEBRATE LIFE

What I want
is to celebrate life
in a garden of tulips,
to laugh long and sit idly
dipping my feet into a pool,
to run naked in the wind
and find others out there
to do it with me.

What I want
is to celebrate life
not death,
to have a home large enough
to let in the cockroach
and stranger together,
a home with running water
and daffodils to put on the feet
of the weary,
a home where the hungry of the world
sip cocoa thirty times a day
or more if needs be.

What I want
is to let my crippled self
be danced over
by the wing of a butterfly,
to own my weariness
and let my limp hands
be oiled by someone other than me,
then at the end of day
to fall backwards
into a tropical wind
and know my Friend will be there.

FLUTE PLAYER

Your touch
invades me like the dawn
and I run
with the flute
of a shepherd in me.

Oh earth, I say,
land, sea, and sky,
all burdens cease
when I bear the wonder
of You!

SELF PORTRAIT

Eileen
   solo singer
     backwoods girl
extend to us
   a trail
     of your long root,
show us the tree
   from which you were made.

Conceal not
   the branch
     of your hanging,
the rope
   whose shreds
     you live by.

Be for us
   a sign
     of delivery,
a Stream
   running through
     the city of our concerns.

Achevé d'imprimer en novembre 1998 chez

IMPRESSION À DEMANDE INC.

à Boucherville, Québec